houses

are

fields

houses
are
fields

poems

Taije Silverman

 LOUISIANA STATE UNIVERSITY PRESS   BATON ROUGE

Published with the assistance of the Sea Cliff Fund

Published by Louisiana State University Press
Copyright © 2009 by Taije Silverman
All rights reserved
Manufactured in the United States of America
LSU Press Paperback Original

Designer: Laura Roubique Gleason
Typefaces: Garamond Premier Pro and Mrs. Eaves

Library of Congress Cataloging-in-Publication Data
Silverman, Taije, 1974–
    Houses are fields : poems / Taije Silverman.
        p. cm.
    ISBN 978-0-8071-3408-5 (pbk. : alk. paper)
    I. Title.
    PS3619.I5525H68 2009
    811',6—dc22

                                                        2008032661

The paper in this book meets the guidelines for permanence and durability of the
Committee on Production Guidelines for Book Longevity of the Council on Library
Resources. ⊚

Karen
Gabe
Kia

Always, Everywhere

Desire, you unconquered in war;
Desire, vaulting upon our dear goods;
at night you rest on young girls' gentle smiles
then travel, grazing the deep ocean,
to visit the far dwellers whose houses are fields.
The deathless gods cannot escape,
or humans whose whole life is a day.

—from Sophocles' *Antigone*

Contents

3

I Have Wished for a Word

4

The Spring before Spring

I

Winterless

Listen, No One, They're Sleeping

Clinking sound of metal on glass, what future
would want to remember: she began

to shake, in her arm this time, up top, near
the back, where I rubbed. Is it too much,

I asked. *Yes.* Are you okay? *Yes.*
We lose track of answers and questions.

And then her whole arm shaking,
tiny tremors, it could have been anything,

it could have been nothing,
it was nothing, it was always nothing.

Do you want a Xanax?
Half a Xanax.

Then the cheek and the swelled skin
under, and the pink chin, trembling.

Liquid drops on the top fridge shelf, in the door, go
quick, but I don't want to leave you alone up here.

My mother is two words.
Is the sky and the life, the daily world.

Lake of changelings, dreamtime.
Is my mother, is color, is falling and pleasure.

Did you swallow it?
Can you swallow it?

Calling my father's name.
Screaming my father's name.
Grab the phone, beg the ring, screaming.

Can we get your father?

He's outside on the back deck in his one chair,
staring at dusk while it's leaving.

I put my body over hers to stop it.
Quiet down.

Is it happening, she stumbles, the words stuck
as she bites her tongue, voice

thick, ripped.
Yes. It is starting to happen.

When does it end? What day would you trade
for a nightmare? If you could trade—just one.

None. I smack the glass with my knuckles, knock.
Now. I don't speak, let him see, so quick, break

my heart, back deck, anyone. Please.
I'm trying to find the stronger drug, go up, I say, I'll bring it.

Throw sticks of butter onto the floor,
loose pills, empty the shelves, I don't

want to leave you alone.
Anything could happen, anything would.

Her warm skin, the flat sleep
that takes her in, do you want

me to keep reading, *yes*
are you still awake, are you

with me, are you following this

It Was a Good Day

When we imagine someone asking us,
the answer is sadness. But what I think first
is this nightgown, the dark red silk
and my washed hair, that slow lull of space
before sleeping. My mother's rash
is not the first thought. It spreads and loosens,
climbs her face, the bumps blur and I tell her
that it's leaving. It is leaving.
Fear slicks down to size so that time
takes over: beef tenderloin with sugar snaps,
the lemon's aftertaste. *This,* my father says,
pointing to the potatoes, *this is really good.*
My sister pulls three kinds of cookies
out of the freezer and my father asks
Didn't we choose not to have cookies anymore?
Yes, my sister says, *and I chose not to hear that.*
The cookies are halved, passed around,
we claim favorites and tell my sister to take
the cookies away, then not to take them away.
We are laughing. I say to my father
as he eats, *I love you,* and he says, *I love you all,*
the three of us he is able to watch at the counter
in our sweaters and hair, bending and talking
as if skin were a grace. I take a bath.
My mother reads in bed and reads on the toilet,
looking up when I look at her and smiling.
The rash will pass. It was a good day.
My father coughing now. Yawning.

Blackout

We walk home from dinner to find the street dark
and we try to remember streetlights. Anything is possible.

The hallway curves inward to cradle lit candles.
                Walls shake with light. The house looks

familiar again, like the right dream.
        I move between rooms lighting candles,

      carrying them upstairs.
My mother's curls have gotten longer.

Her nightgown makes a tent around her shoulders.
       I love you so much, she says. I forget everything.

I forget the dream where her voice
            is her old voice and where

      when she hugs me goodnight, all of her is there,
answering yes of course and always when I ask for it.

Good night, god bless, sweet no we won't
       sleep I have pressed my face down to the floor

of the bathroom where my mother fell one year ago
         more than a year ago now we never

      say it. Karen, my father said. Oh Karen
and I walked in slowly and saw and I picked up the phone.

I held her. For how long? For how long did I hold her?
      Someone answer. For how long did I hold her.

      Now my father walks into the bathroom and sharply
breathes *What*—Everything's fine, I say and stand up.

Mommy? He asks, and I start to sob.
Shhh, he says, so she won't hear me. *Shhh.*

and I say why is this happening to us.

Why is this happening is what you ask
but you keep walking through rooms to relight the candles.
If you can see something, you think,
you can see enough.

The edge of a table. The glass of water
on the kitchen counter that someone forgot.

Stand still in a room lit by candlelight:
the corners look larger. You can't see

where things end. There must be more space
than you'd ever expected.

Past the bricks in the mantel, on the other side
of the couch, where the dark starts.

There must be more space.
Stand still.

Letter to Mandelstam

You still haven't died, you're still not alone
      starts a poem you wrote the last winter
before your arrest. No one learned
      the true date of your death. Here
         it's summer, and warm, even this late

at night, and I think you've been dead now
      too long for these scrawled words to reach you.
Osip! Your joy is still rising
      as heat rises up from the earth.
         While walking this morning

to work through the park I imagined you
      walking down Voronezh streets, past the faces
of strangers like memories, keeping their distance.
      I passed flowerbeds filled with shrugged bunches
      of mint, sage the color of dust

and beneath a collapsed trunk of ivy,
      two trumpet vine blooms. Trumpet vine
is that flower that looks more like fire,
      or some crazed angel's horn, which all
      summer in stem-laden choirs

will climb through the city. It's the same kind
      I brought to my mother's first room
at the brain tumor center,
      fourth floor, room nine, though I'd find her
      at rehab, relearning to use her left side.

Osip, wait—I had wanted to write
      about trumpet vine blooms, not the ones
that I left by a hospital bed but this morning's
      improbable flames. Last night
      it must have rained. And maybe

you haven't been dead for too long
            because even near dawn, I'm awake,
forcing words to the fugitive tune
            (*stolen air,* you once wrote)
                        that your disappeared walks

will still move to: brash boys with toboggan sleds
            slung by their hips, foreign countries of ice
shifting under the bridge, and the imprints
            in mud left by horses, then half-filled
                        with rain. You stepped your tall boot in

and named their shape, saying *This
            is memory.* Meaning all of these moments
of beauty are moments of change. And change
            was the unyielding charge brought
                        against you, all evidence plain

in the ice pressed to horseshoes: you knew
            it would thaw, and that soon
you'd be sent for by strangers.
            And when the small doctor I do not believe
                        says my mother will live for another two years,

well of course I would choose to stop time.
            But I can't imagine it.
Would we freeze the way kids do,
            mid-stride in their grave games of freeze tag?
                        And what about sunset?

I remember sunsets past Crossroads Store
            that could drop the bottom lip: silver ships,
dragon tails, orange silk swathed
            across blue hills on a sky, I swear,
                        that had to be alive

and my mother and I would sit on the curb
        and stare, thinking only *luck,* and *luck,* and *love,*
and how soon we should drive home, to begin dinner.

If You're Asking

My father sees cable television as a cure for cancer.
Right now Adam Sandler is teaching a six-year-old
how to seduce the waitress in a sports bar

and my father is laughing heartily under covers.
My mother leans gently toward the edge of the bed, intent
on the screen, though I know she isn't watching.

Things are good. Things are unthinkable.
Yes, I can tell every well-meaning neighbor: she is healing.
Or yes, I can say: She's a lovely stranger. She's a child I love.

The last of the crape myrtle's blooming. Hot pink petals
on pavement like romance found after the party.
Some last record, spinning the last slow dance.

Cicadas make the sound of metal. *It's their wings,*
my mother explained, *they're rubbing their wings together.*
I looked *cicada* up in our children's encyclopedia: it's a muscle

in the abdomen, not wings. But when I hear them
I hear her voice, and don't question. *Their wings.*
Such sturdy rage, like trains meant for a strange

distance but speeding instead toward the wrong central station
where every window and destination will instantly shatter.
Then later: crickets like a sack of silver necklaces.

Before dusk we ducked through a window upstairs
where, on the balcony, a hammock collects spiders and twigs.
Twice we tried climbing it without falling and failed,

falling, and laughing. My mother's left arm pinned
to my ribs, toes stuck in the net which stretched willfully.
I just peed, she said laughing. *Oh shit,* I said laughing.

The sky this wild, shy pink above John's house,
and First Street already dissolving. Black mosquitoes,
and patience. *Have you gotten used to this,* my father asked

one morning when I found him alone in the basement
with another cigarette. *In the sense that you can get used
to anything,* I said and he nodded: *Good answer.*

My Father's Unhappiness

At night in the swept yellow gleam of the kitchen
I sit with my father and watch while he eats

I offer a secret or ask for a story
it must be the milk glass that won't let him speak

he stares at me hard I
stare at him please it's my heart

my eyes promise him he won't believe he says
you cannot never will know what I need

is the throat of the dark past the deck in the garden,
the memory death spits on children being born

is the one that once challenged regret and it won
so regret like a god became jealous

My father's unhappiness is a curse. Is a gift.

is the blue sleeve of the long afternoon
the locked space in the gut of the whale

is the trailing of air down the stairs in the mornings
the front door swung open hey folks he will call

is the weight of love lasting love calls for this lasting
love fills up the milk glass says here's what you need

I say drink it he spits I say sorry he leaves
I say love you he says it right back oh the air

and right now he is sleeping slow burn by my mother
their bed always wider and white onto white.

Inheritance. I hold you like a bird. Your bones in my fingers.
Bird bones, buried in the yard.

Are You the God

Regret. I give you up like a shoe.
A woman's sandal. The bent sole.
I give you up like a dead whale, sand
screened to its belly and stinking.
I give you as sun on the summer's hottest day.
I give you like plates of food for the starving,
killed by the sudden enough.
I give you up like a blade.
I give you as blue on the cheek blush
of Krishna, playing, blue of the dusk
before night comes. You are the glow we remember.
The brightest of light leaving, the dance we make.
You are the god, not the gift for the god.
And you are tender I think. You would
be merciful with me. Bright piece
of a field, just once in the afternoon, I picked flowers.
The forest kept its own smell and I named it,
hidden witness, seal of dampness and bark.
I am at your feet. I give my heart to you, for lifting.
Is it you who will absolve? Kindness of skin.

Element

You sit cross-legged against my bedroom floor,
recounting some old rage the way

we sometimes talk of rage to try to keep it.
Your forehead strains to shape the words.

What can I say? I'd look at you all summer if I could.
Your eyes are light and hard. I ask if you think things

will ever change. You tell me no. So while
you talk I daydream years ago: the week

my cousin's father died, she'd yelled at me.
I'd washed her sheets—the blue had bled.

If I want help, my cousin said, I'll ask for help.
That night we walked down to the river, stood

by reeds that had grown taller than our heads.
In her low voice I love, my cousin asked if I would please

forgive her. I had forgiven her the moment that she yelled.
What choice do we have, beneath anger?

But something stayed—some hurt, or shame.
It must have seeped in through the bottoms of my feet.

And now it's in me, I explained, but I forgive you.
My cousin wrapped her hands around the roots

of several reeds, then slid her fingers up until
she'd cupped the feathered seed inside her palms.

She held it out to me. The seed was pale,
and had no weight. It was as soft as sleep.

Tonight an hour will have passed before you lift
your gaze to ask—*How did I start to talk about all that?*

Your story has you by the limbs. As mine has me.
I bring my finger to your mouth, and whisper *sand,*

then move it out to touch your cheek.
It's an element kiss, I say, not knowing

more than you do what I mean. I reach again.
Your lips come loose to close around my finger.

Air. The body doesn't know its love.
Your other cheek I kiss to *snow.*

The scar beside your chin is made of *fire.* The skin
between your lovely eyebrows: *dirt.* I wish my kisses

could dissolve you. I wish that what we wanted
could be offered up, instead—loose fists

packed full of feathers, culled from seed drift
in a river—pulled to gather, helpless, held.

The Winter Before

My mother knocked on the bathroom door
to read me a poem. Her happiness was shining.
Even now, she read from her place on the page,
the Beloved is tending himself inside of you.
When I didn't smile she asked, *Isn't it beautiful?*
God is inside of us. For no reason I remembered
my dream from the night before, how I had no money
in a strange city and each male friend I asked
for a place to stay wanted sex in return.
No reason. I smiled. I let her happiness
be my happiness, which is easy sometimes,
but when she turned to walk toward
her bedroom, I wanted to call to her: *Wait.*
All my dreams had come back.
Dreams of being alone in strange cities,
a man following or being followed—death
as the lover we greet indifferently, on the stairs.
Wait. I wanted to ask her, *Will we be all right?*
My father was already sleeping in the bed
she would climb into and the skin on their bodies
was the most precious thing I would ever know.
I would lose it. *Will we be all right?* The door
closed *click,* shut. All the ghosts in the hallway exhaled.
Inside me somewhere buried and lightless
I was sobbing and would not stop, but in the mirror
my eyes were dry. I asked to forget and to be
forgiven, though I asked no one, and nothing.

Let's Pretend We Are

When would it become real?
You asked the pillows in a perfect tense.

As if this were something you wanted.
Playing around, touching the real while it sleeps.

Hey. Whispering. *I'm going upstairs.* It won't wake.
Or: *Watch me now, I'm in the room, the sheets
her body died on are the palest blue.*

Nothing, not a start.

But you can tell the difference between death and sleep. The air
refuses your name: *I am a thing, it explains. You—
are a memory.* None of the birds sigh.

Your father walks in while you circle the body.
I just saw a shooting star, he says.
Everything makes sense to me now.

But this stretching and looping of time. So you move
backwards. In the morning the sky at the top of the block
was a bright, new blue.

This smoothing down. This gravity, enlarging.
Your father walks rooms filled with vases of flowers.

Walking round and around, you think this
was your life, and you did have it, and you did know it would go.

The real floats off, no hurry, no reason.
That was a sky, this
was a life, you walk

through the house in the beautiful roses of aftermath, laughing.
Unknown to yourselves and so fearless.

What would you prod, to wake up? Oh nothing, not for the world.

You spread your palm across her forehead
and stroked it, sometimes the motion made her close her eyes.
You wished sleep for her. You wished anything.

2

In the Late Night

Letter to Send

We're making love when I ask you what the future is like. *The future?* you ask. Our room is a cupboard of shadows. *The future is fun,* you say. *I like it!* I ask you if it's big. *Big? No. It's deep. Like a tunnel,* you tell me. *A very long tunnel.*

I think of the drives we used to take when I was a child, of the tunnels that led through mountains surrounding our city. My sister and I would hold our breath and press both hands onto the roof of the car until we'd reached the other side. Only this, our parents claimed, could keep the tunnels up.

In bed I ask you if the tunnel has an ending. *Everything has an ending,* you say. Sometimes I wonder if you could answer all my questions. My love. My warm, one stranger. It's late now. At dawn my father will wake me and I will stumble into the next room, take his place in the bed beside my mother. Everything has an ending. My sister and I, as children: that first, exhaled, rush of breath. And the shape of the tunnel is an arc, so that we see light, and not what we are leaving.

Here

Put out your hands. Take static, the fuzzed edge
of the intercom, catching waves. I listen to her breathing.

Put out your hands, stupid future, I am giving you her breathing.

Her awake, in the dark room, the plush
bed, blues and reds, the warmth of her head
beside tents of pillows.
I press my face.

Here: her breath
is a rustle beneath static,
is a long, inhaled rope.
It catches twice, on spirit or exhaustion.

The soundtrack of background noise,
a shuffled sheet, a padded foot, it isn't hers, my father sleeps
his earth of weight through every coated
whispering. *Is it Taije?* Yes.

Her face is a broad, sleek shape of bones.
Her darkest eyes, white skin, her warmth, gains elegance.

Hold me. You, my mother whose arm is gone,
while it's here, hold me so I press

my self right to you. *It's pretty nice that—*
It's pretty nice that what? *That—*

Memory, scoop us up. The sounds we make,
not sleeping yet, still dreaming out of time.

Pick us up. Bring us through. We're waiting here, we want you.

Letter to Have, Letter to Hold

What will the world be like, I ask my therapist. You mean—she says. And I say yes. What is it like, when it's motherless. She tells me: you love more. And I say what is there to love. I say it like I'm shrieking. Things, she answers. Neutrinos. She looks at me. I really mean that, she says.

In bed I tell you how neutrinos are so small, they can move through lead without leaving a trace. How it's only from water that we know they exist. They rearrange the water's structure. Scientists bury boxes of water inside mountains and under the ocean, then dig them up later for evidence. You, I explain, are a neutrino. *But that's small,* you say, in quick protest. *I want to stick.*

Our love is a skin, is a smell. We are all touch. *I'm a proton,* you argue. *I'm at the center!* I laugh at you, this rich delight. You're a neutrino, I say. You're a trace. I am water, I tell you, and you are my trace.

The Way It Falls

You're awake for no reason in the middle of the night,
and the type of each letter looks forceful. Your body
keeps a secret, you don't speak. How many selves
in one imperative. How complete, the absence of question.
You're awake for no reason in the middle of the night.
The intercom runs a steady static, soft as a rustle
smoothed over. Beneath it the oxygen tank hums.
Put it to a three, your mother says, in a voice
you keep secret. You turn the tank on, let the sound
of it starting slice air. You turn the lamp on. A black bug
flares off the ceiling, crazy crepe paper, crazy fear.
Your body keeps a secret limned in sweetness.
Listen, this is what she needs. To sit up for a moment.
You worry for her neck, without your hand, the way
it falls, and what supports it's you you're not enough.
Keep this a secret. She knows. The left side of her body
has been shaking. Does she want? A sip of water.
The water sticks again inside her throat. Her chest, yes.
Your body knows the answer to a question.
Your body knows the question is an absence.
You rub her arm, and hot left hand, you bring
the lotion downward, from her shoulder.
You love her arm. Your one and only huge imperative.
You bring the heat down, outward, through your fingers.
It lessens, so. You shake it from your fingers and it travels
to your lungs. You'd die for what. You think there
in the dark with her how secretly you know it's you.
And does Taije have a brain tumor, too?
your grandmother asks, on the back deck.
She holds your mother's hand, the left, and no one knows
what comfort brings, or takes. They are each other's
former loves. They are each other's promises,
broken and kept. *I'm dying Mom,* she tells her, on the deck.
Your father clears his throat, he doesn't sleep.
You think you hear them talking through the wall.
You're hearing nothing, all the time, soft voices.

Letter to Burn

In tonight's hotel room you reach for me and whisper, *You're a pacifier.* But what I hear is *piece of fire.* I nod into your neck, yes: I am a piece of fire. So this is love, I think, this misunderstanding: you pressed to me like a baby sucking itself to sleep while I burn to bits from the inside, smolder out from my smallest part.

I'm mad, I tell you. *At me?* At everything. *You sure at everything, and not at me?* I ask you what's the difference. You slap my face. I slap back, my loose hand lunging for a landing place. You slap me harder and I'm surprised by the shape my fist makes, as if my hand had moved to fight without me. The hits are hard and quick but the time between seems slowed: enough to think, between blows, how I could lie down at the foot of this bed and just wait for you to wreck me. Piece of fire. I am straw burning, a mess of smoke. I know only that I should stay in the fight, in order to end it.

I jump on you, surprise attack. You flip us back to smash against the bedspread. My legs climb up the length of you, to lock around your head. You bite my shin. This body of anger I live in. This misunderstanding. I bring my hand to touch your face, still locked in place above me. Then draw it down to mine, and kiss your lips. Pacifier. You are all health and flushed limbs, breathing. I pull your head down gently now, and press it to my breasts. And stroke your hair, and listen to you catch your breath.

Look, There

Wall of air. Cheek place. Do this, do this.
What's grief then, you can't sustain it.

Her body has a warmth that comes
from under the skin, isn't heat

the way our other moving bodies
give off heat but hers

is swirling. Simmer. Slow, hold.
She's lying in the bed, she's alone.

She's stayed outside until dark again,
on the back deck, though the air is getting colder.

She's in the bed there. I spread the red shawl,
take this sip of water, are you—

What's that word before sweetness.
What's that word before.

But we've been upstairs for hours, it's too
cold outside, already the next season, look.

What I don't understand is forever.
That her going means gone. Will go.

What's the difference, the bloom asks the bloom.
That her going—

Look, fall's here. See how the leaves—?
So that's how it happens, I say, pretending.

She's sleeping in their bedroom, he's beside her,
his outline ending, so that's how—

He fell asleep with his glasses on,
the book opened over his chest.

I pulled it from his hand that sleeping held it.
He made a sound, he didn't wake.

In the dark his glasses were little moons.
In the dark he had fallen asleep.

You can think about the circles of hell.
The future. The lovers. The weather.

You can say it in circles, do this.
She might be sleeping. She might be—

here in the memory's morning.
You heard her voice, and clearly.

Hi T, she calls from her pillow.
Hi Ma! you call back, from yours.

Letter without a Word

We're lying in bed and the rain is a strange sound. I've never heard it. Making love there's an instant when I stop thinking, then with gratitude for the instant I begin again. I ask if you could be strong enough for both of us. If you could live for me. Draw up a contract that binds you for good to me. Give me your earlobes, and neck. *Yes,* you respond, to every request. Your love stretches like elastic, then snaps back. I'm having a hard time, I say. Do you know that?

But the look on your face is from a dream that I haven't had. I want to refuse it. You mean, I ask, this isn't the hard time? You say nothing. This isn't it, I repeat. Your eyes are a child's eyes, that grave. It's still coming, I say, isn't it. You nod your head. Then I'm sobbing. Then I'm pressed to your body because it's the only one here. This isn't it, I keep saying, like a mimic. The words close in my throat like a cast of the shape they negate.

Though it's everywhere. No longer the nightmare but the neighborhood streets. Still can't speak. *Ever ever ever,* says the echo. *Ever,* says the stir of dust. Just: this rain, I don't recognize. A sound hitting hard matter like—what?

A Softer Creature

Hey white sheets hey quiet night.
Hey swans, in another country.

Hey hurricanes. Before bed my father says
your mother makes everyone into dwarves.
My mother yawns. *See,* my father says,
she is making me shrink right now!

Hey skyscrapers falling hey rainstorm of rubble.
Hey, dreamt-up disaster.

I could go downstairs, I could pull in the shadows
for my fever. Pull in the landing
where the moon falls down.
I could go downstairs. No farther.

Someone is singing, somewhere else. I hear things.
I could not ever leave the house.

Today I read a poem about preparing for death.
But the poem was a warning, and what use is that.
Fear is a softer creature now, he wants
to get to know us. He is also afraid.

Her face fails, twitches for minutes
before I open my eyes. We are with fear now, waiting.

He's a guest, like us. And no one knows
what's to come.

Siren's Letter

Tonight Venus came out early, as it does sometimes. Blazed like an accident above our back deck while my father sat smoking his last cigarette, and my mother waited upstairs in the bedroom. We say I love you most times without thinking, but the words always hang behind. They are gaining resistance to gravity. And you can feel how thick the air gets, like a mattress—everything lying down on it or sliding.

Right now: people are laughing on another street. They must be drunk. Beside me is a letter that says love in itself is no virtue. I am a riddle of disbelief. A chalkboard. If you were here tonight I would make you kiss an exact spot on the back of my neck. Any spot, but that one exactly.

A friend asked why I love you and I said because my love for you will end. If it's enough, or not enough—I don't have to wonder. Come home, I can say, and be calling you to air. To a space the size of a jar, where fireflies shine. Your neck for my lips, my thumb for your cheek. I am your own last hour of dreaming, and you must find me.

October

Always the dream inside the dream.
I lay down in the carpeted lobby.
Insisted my failure was a statement, look.
I am taking myself out of the picture.

And the homes people lived in, like musical chairs.

All day in bits. We slept. My face
to her neck to her cheek to her shoulder her

skin is the sun's secret heat. I press in, we sleep.
I love this picture, someone says, having come to see.
That one? No, she says, framing. This.
My mother is warm, we make each other sleepy.

Through the window the maple is losing its leaves.

But their brave yellow gold hasn't faded, I promise
to strangers in letters, though leaves fall like snow
all day long, to the street. And the street's
piling up like a river.

Down toward the end of the block, that new distance.

Now the leaves have curled to fingers
and they've lost their yellow color.
It doesn't matter what I think about time, what I wish for.
This cause and effect is a myth.

Of course I was trying to save her, in the dream.
It was no different from failing. Ever.

Her Sleep, His Sleep, and I Am Filled

I am thinking of a lover who is thinking of the future.
I am wanting those hands in my hair.

Here both my parents are sleeping.
My mother sleeps: a new sleep, not known
by the name of sleep but as water that won't hold weight.
Known by the name of fall's husks, by the name
of the unremembered—memories. Boys with limp limbs
and their voices like birds dying, stretched from the branches
of trees, behind my boarding school. Now that was a dream.
Moon shapes under the harmless one's eyes, the cool light.
Now that was a memory. She is sleeping a sleep
known by names in wells. It skims the surface, weightless.
She doesn't dream, my mother says. But she is dreaming.
My lover's name, his child's name, the name
like bells my lover's wife. *He was going—*
back to them, she explains. *It's right.*
But her eye won't stop bleeding, she's fallen from the bed. Trying
to reach them. *It's right.* My father drives five miles to the one
drugstore still open, buys the special kind of cloth we must press
to her head. He must press—he must not—let me do this.
He is thinking of a lover who is thinking of the future.
For a while she cried all the time. Films where all daughters
would dance at their weddings—on the brink, it seemed—
of giving birth. My mother sobbing. She is sleeping.
My father sleeping. A light sleep. There is no dream safe enough.
I come to lift her and he's awake again, or he has been awake
for days, or years, though he sleeps in hospital chairs, foldout cots,
the bedroom's piled pillows for whatever movie we must watch—
together. He falls asleep, he's snoring. *I'll just take*
a quick nap, he says, in the middle of the day. The nap is draped
in lace. His sleep is known by the name of sleep. It is a hand,
and holds him. When he wakes up he will not wake up. Nothing
will wake him up. Not the sound of her fall, not *what happened?*
Go back to sleep the covers mumble to him, sleep.

I am wanting to lie by my lover at night. And when I wake up
I don't know him, and I hold him, like we're one body, changing shape.

The Last Letter

Little by little, my mother tells me, and I tell her no. I am the one who sobs and slobbers, the one with her head on the pillow. I am the one who screams, Why are you leaving me? You said you wouldn't. *I can't help it,* she tells me. *Please,* she says. *Don't beg.*

Try to imagine. Like imagining rain, with no knowledge of rain. The first three years of my life were a drought. I cried, my first rainfall. Not from fear exactly but—how can I say it? We didn't get enough time.

And you, who insisted, my stranger. My spinning star, my spark. You wanted to come in. Welcome. Take the blame, if you love me. Cede me your body parts. Let me carry your scalp in my pocket, or quit all your claims. Fool. Don't you understand that my mother is leaving my father? They sobbed for each other. Always, finally, for each other. Will you miss him? I ask. *Yes.* But you'll be dead, I argue, so you won't miss him. *I'll stay human for a little while after,* she says. *Isn't that what happens?* You'll be dirt, I tell her. You'll be dead.

She says *It's love that's important. It's love that brings everything together.* No, I say. It's love that breaks everything apart. *That's how it brings everything together,* she says. *You know that. You've been in love.*

Disappearing bumblebee, the back steps. Nighttime trees, just past the deck. Welcome. You wanted to come in. It's the ending. It's the memory, that fits like skin.

Take the blame. If you love me. *You know that,* she says. *You've been in love.* Memory of crying, that fits like skin. The name for rain. Yellow boots, the first time. Windowshine. Motherlove. Ending. What's to come? Nightfall.

3

I Have Wished for a Word

Fugue

It started with my mother
     using the walker to get from her bedside to the bathroom
and me saying wow, and wonderful.

It started one morning
     when my mother looked in the mirror and asked: Who
the fuck is that? Disgusted.

It started with the medicines:
     the ones that make her cheeks swell up,
the ones that make her hair fall out in tufts.

She asks us now to brush it straight, all day.
She wants it gone. She hands us nests
of hair left on the sheets.

It started
     when the gods came out of their tin huts, pounding.
Someone, somewhere, has made a mistake.

And here in the mirror
my mother's face
     is a ball of dough. Who

the fuck. Do you know

you're you, I asked, underneath it? No.

It started when I told my mother
     to look at me. It started with the pause,
before she did. Somewhere, someone.

Do you know you're you
     who loves me? I asked, and started it. That long before
she answered, I don't know.

It started when I told her, well I *do*.
  It started when I promised, when I lied. I thought I could find
her eyes. I thought I could look, from mine, and tell them.

Good, she said. So . . .
  where's my toothbrush?
I handed her the toothbrush. She brushed her teeth.
For years we were silent at the mirror, listening to the bristles push.

When she walked
  out of the bathroom her legs buckled.
So it started, when I didn't say stop. Come back to me. Walk.

I dragged a chair to the door with one hand, dragged
  my mother from the walker down into it.

  My father walked into the room. What's happening folks.
It started when he failed. Do you know you're you.

I said Mom doesn't recognize herself.
  Here, Mom. You sit and talk with Dad about it.
It started when they talked about it.

What you need, he told her, is a different shirt.
  Like this red one, he said, and they were one person, failing.

And then it started, on the staircase, when he dropped her.

When he screamed my name. When I dropped the phone.

He could not lift her up again, or let her fall.

My mother on the third step, in the red blouse.

I slipped my arms beneath her arms and dragged her up to standing.
  I don't remember her shaking completely
but she was shaking completely.

Listen, I said. Please. Will, I said. Do.
  It started with me speaking. We walked each step.
Her knees held. Wow, we said. Wonderful. We kept her up.

We swept her up. We wept her—Please.
  It started when we finished, when we got downstairs.
You did it, you—Beautiful. It started one morning.

She looked in the mirror. My father
  dropped her, on the steps.
It started when.

We're in the living room, my mother's
  lips are parted. She's too tired to. My mother leaning
into the cushions of the couch. It started

when we got there. My mother looking at me, from someplace
  I can't see. I see: my mother's face, puffed to dough
around her features. I see the starting point, shift through time.

So when she turns to me on the couch and asks,
  Would you let me go?
It hasn't come yet. We're still nowhere, we haven't arrived.

When she turns to my soul from a place I can't see.
  Would you let me
                    go?

Could it have started with the question?
  No.
My mother, one morning, leaning into the couch. The late light.

Little by Little (I)

Voices in the kitchen, high low   the door
                                 open, slide
of the cup across table, rage   the gold
                               sandals
                               slip, open
Leaf   shake,
                light   gone
Go
No

In the room through the window   open, memory
on the green cloth, the table, long
                         light, moves
                         on the hand, mine she is
                             sleeping

There's no form to this   water
in the lake under stars no   reflection

You heard rain, a long
                     time ago, open

Bird call in another yard is the rib's
insistence

Bird call in another yard asking what
                           have I done for you
the small
wing, breastbone
she's tired   and so
                 talking
a green tree
a what
a tree   a what

green tea with leaves
        a tree with leaves   a tree with leaves with
oh   so she's
                rooted

there's a place at the end, he said, *you want to tell them—go,*
be new again

you were my hand
my light
fingers, in light

every piece, leaf
something's
touching

Picture (his arms around, their black and white)
wherever you go, my father says,
                    my love goes—that's
                                        for   ever

pink blanket the wool
one this fringe
                    Are you cold

by: bird rattle and
bird weight, little
lifting, this
sound, of the day, of, this sound   rustle, by

How could I let you—

wing lift

Be back in a—
(while, baby)
            (what's
                        a while)

copper-lit   rooftop,
little   rain-net, slide   by   little by

voices

To Be, Afraid

It is a moment, your teacher says
of the poem "To Autumn" but it does happen in time.
There is late, and there is later.

Season of delight. You can almost feel, he says,
that if it has to end, then this is the way . . . surely he pauses.

In the night your lover likes to ask
how you would meet your death.

I would fight it to the last second, he says.
I would stagger to the bathroom on even
my last morning to shave.

A lover's touch is like a mother's touch, someone says,
but it isn't. A lover's touch is a child's.

How you will meet your death is your myth. Your youth.

Your sister calls you on the train. There is late, and—
Mom was asleep, she says, but
her eyes were open. She wouldn't wake.

Late, and later and late, and later, and what
will you do for Thanksgiving, and when
will your mother die, and how
in the future is this going to be worse.

Were you afraid that it wouldn't end? Of course.

The question is one of risk, your teacher explains.
A kind of—vulnerability, to the moment.
It's a terrible thing, he says, to be interrupted.

The hospice nurse believes
that in the afterlife, we can function without fear.
Late, and later.

One morning between drifts your mother says clearly,
I am not going to be afraid.

Keats wrote "To Autumn" into the future of time, propelling it
forward, into, toward. To this, we say, and go.
Where the gaze is. She said it twice.
In her room. On a recent morning.

Between bits of word shapes, slurred speech.
I am not going to be afraid.

You slept with your arms holding her arm, and your face
touching her shoulder and cheek, and you heard
her speak, but you felt no need to wake.

Little by Little (the time)

Little by little the time goes *where* we ask
      looking for places. Little.

By the graveyard names the years
      in stone a husband's wife who chose the word
            beloved. Little.

The unnamed grass along
      the edge *I wouldn't mind*

        something like this says my sister we're walking
            through quiet, apart.
            Up ahead our dad's black leather jacket.

We're thinking the one thing, we're thinking
        the no thing, we're thinking weather.

Little by little the day. Little by little the warmth.
If she were here, we don't think. She is here.

By little by
      come, to the room *would you*
        cover me stranger
        me cover me up with a blanket? Thanks.

She's my mother's—skin, by little, would you—
no, would you, yes, could you, how, you
      will, little by little.

We're walking *home is wherever you*
            and Daddy are by
               little and here

               winter
            air, it's time
       for humidifiers, I might say,
          the candles in windows, warm
             milk with its one spoon of honey.

We are this big, we are this shape, we are this
                        point on this place *Look!* I can—
                        no she's not seeing this at all.
How slow change is.
                We took naps, at one and nine.
You looked so sweet, my father said, *I didn't*
                        want to wake you. Is that all right?
                It's nice. Was I pressed up next to Mom?

Yes. Right here, he says, showing.

Little by little the birdseed
Little by little the silver pole, a pathway
by swallows the old willow by
barn doors bowed open by
ghosts that speak words without sound
and stay out where they lived by the
loved skin, in grass, the stones:
names, drawn, the ghosts
kept to their places the barn's arc gleam
or held rooms I still dream
the ghosts fine I still, time

Who Are We That We Come from Somewhere Else

In the gazebo we sit facing each other, and I play out
the question eight times before asking.

Can I ask you a question?

It comes out garbled and shy
but the girl looks up quick and says yes.

And her hand rests
on the back of the bench, and it's near

my chin, and for some long, clean
instant I think what if I could have anything I wanted.

I bring my chin to her hand. What if. I could have
anything.

Her hair and eyes, her rounded
nose, her voice like fishhooks, catching.

What if. My lips
reach out of me to kiss her neck's

dipped center. It's like her heart, this part of her,
the circled drain that pulls the sink's white bowl.

She's breathing hard. I'm choosing this,
and helpless to it, leaning.

We walk back to the house with hardly any gravity.
There is the darkness that takes away our hands

but now a mist cuts through it. Mist moves
through the woods like a fabric, slides

screens between trees and falls
to the road in long columns, collapsing.

Something silent and giant is alive with us.
It will not speak, but it wants to be gentle.

I am thinking about Dante, about the souls who live
inside fire. They had refused to believe in an afterlife.
Now they are lost to it, taken as if kidnapped from time.

I am thinking of my uncle and how he came
to my cousin in a dream, after his death.
It was real, she told me, and I grieved for her.

I am thinking of my mother's father who died two days ago.
We don't miss him, we don't know what we've lost.

I am thinking how if there is an afterlife
then this is it, this mist we have found here by accident.

We stop on the road to watch.

White neck, white birch, white drifting.

I am tall, and I reach my arms around her.
She fits inside me like a birch tree.

Still staring at the mist she says
You know, for a long time I felt gripped by sadness.

I am thinking of my mother,
vomiting up the second round of chemotherapy.

She bursts a blood vessel and gets a black eye.
I want to answer, *yes.* For a long time.

And I don't, anymore, she says, turning. *I just realized that.*

I know she is telling the truth, as if it had just happened.
Mist keeps slipping loose between the trees.
Her body is so light in my arms.

In the Afterlife

It's true: your mother's breathing.

What you have to do, someone explains,
is walk past a grave.

You hear the ease in that voice
like a knife through bread.

Your mother's breathing.

Are those small black birds
up there swallows you ask.

Why would a soul say I don't know.
Why would a soul use words.

Don't go, don't go, or so
the poem starts, but the author is talking to God.

What they forget to say: when you sit on the edge
of her bed at night, you're in the afterlife.

How the dark of the bedroom gives way:
shadows to moonlight like water to shore,

the curled gate at the mouth of the cave,
how you will always wait there.

Listen, listen: waves. The cave as a rock,
opened up. The rock as a shape-shifting door.

You don't need to remember.

Mosquito

Let's say memory is at the mercy of gravity.
Let's say gravity has a mercy. *Here,* it says,
in our mother's voice, *I forgive you.*
Let's say it lets us down slowly, this child
the size of a palm. Infant, body
of bloom smell, and love.
Let's say she takes it in her arms.
Here, like a lifting, and lowered.
As if memory were a kind of matter.
Matter, transformed, into matter.
Makeedo, my mother says, in the bathroom.
Mak-Akido. Aketa. We're down
on our knees, trying to find her.
A word, transformed, into a sound.
Makeeto. Kedo. Let's say the tongue
touches the lips with the gravity light knows,
or suffers from. In its lowering down
around barks of trees. Let's say this was always
a question of longing: something asked for,
something named. Let's say we swam
in that listening, as if—we could have heard,
by listening hard. If something is needed
it must be found. If a substance is made of matter
it will remain matter, matter becoming
matter, we ask back, *Mom?* How many times.
The body lowered. The body fits a mother's palm.
As if gravity were a kind of lifting.
The particle of weight, particle of shape,
particle of *where, here, please.*
We're kneeling before her, we're squatting
on the bathroom floor. We're moving so fast
that no pattern could trace us, we move
in place. Tell me the name, we keep saying.
What you need. Anything. Take
the point of this red pen and make it go all
the way down. *Please.* Not held

above paper but gripped there, oh enemy
unseen. As if gravity were a kind of mercy.
As if matter were at the mercy of gravity.
Oh if. It says. In our mother's voice.
Soft like a windsweep, like singing. Substance
to substance, light to dirt, the God raining.
As if time. Let's say memory.
That we could hold it in our arms.
That she could hold it in her arms. Lower down.
From a kind of distance, to a kind of shape.
Matter to matter, as if made. As if falling. In place.

Little by Little (II)

Little by little we don't sleep, the rain
stops, sound
        in the kitchen
        of laughter is stranger.

What will become of us, in the after.
I ask her:
        do you still believe
that there is, underneath this
        all

           this
           no such thing as leaving?

        Yes.

Little by little: listen.

She rubs my thumbnail smooth against her finger.
She could hold anything, now.
        A rubber sea urchin. The creased edge
        of the duvet cover, to know it.

She holds and then
lets go—she knows
        how I will not go with her.

As if I've refused.

(Why do I think of the customshouse, small
as a room, in the winterland I only know from dreams?
Someone must pass through, must be
                permitted.
The warmth is a way station, these gold windows.
           We don't stay there.)

My father again downstairs, laughing.
She holds my hand. Little by little.

He stays downstairs so late now.

She lets it go. The cover's fold
                    pulled into bulk
                              between my mother's fingers.
This old, and always
                    child's call: what do I have,
                    and is it all
I want?

I Want to Kill the Moths

I can't say: sweat, and then skin, and then mom, and then speak.
No such thing as a sentence, it seems. No such thing
as what's happening. Moth under the covers, get out.
Brown wings, hung on the lamp stand. If the soul lives
in memories then the soul is no matter to reckon with.
Forgettable. I cleaned the shit but didn't get it all.
She whimpered in pain. She said *Stop it right now.*
I told her, I'm sorry. *I don't believe you,* she said.
The bedroom flowers are purple and green, flushed bright
when the window shows dusk on leaves. The big pillows
are wet with sweat. The smaller ones are smeared
with ointment, nests of hair. I dumped dead tulips
in the bathroom. Put water in bottles on windowsills:
dumped the white spray, tucked pink buds of peonies
with the last dark iris from a larger bouquet.
I do anything but stop. It takes all day. I tried to pull her
on the pull sheet by myself. Wish me good luck, I told her.
Luck, she said. I looked at her and she looked at me
and we laughed, and when I couldn't even budge her
we laughed harder. But we were laughing thinking
we are losing this, now. Thinking gone soon.
I want to kill the moths. This afternoon at the end
of the movie where a girl danced with her boyfriend
at a wedding (outside, by a lake, at night) my sister
started sobbing and gripped my mother's leg.
You shouldn't cry, my mother told her, *it isn't good for you.*
When we told her laughing that this was the wrong thing
to say, she told my sister, *You can get snot on my sheet.*
Wiser words of comfort were never spoken, I told my mother,
and she said *I meant it as comfort.* Sentences don't exist.
The you became her. Now everything's over.
The memories are already leaving with the life that made them,
life never made them, it just happened, it's gone.

Covering

So we'll just have to get some of the—
And here is how I know you are missing, and here is where I wait.
We'll just have to get some of the
prompting, raining, question, mark.
You're looking at me from a highway,
the cars, what's moving—this brave

dark. So we'll just have to get some of these
blankets, I tell you, pulling it up. *Yes.*
Color of glowworm, silktent, tucking you in.
Color of keeping you covered.
You'll come back to me. I keep telling you.
I keep asking, in the quiet, will I feel you

with me, when you're gone?
You look and look. Your sweetness.
Color of chewed-up straw ends, your teeth
at my fingers, the color
of colors that change on leaves.
I squeeze your hand between mine

till it stills, it will not still. You scratch
your head, scratch my fingers, press
the rims from my nails till they hurt, find out.
Did you know I slept beside you last night? We didn't sleep.
I held on to your sweet, talking body, its language
of planets in a drift, thick.

After hours of snoring my father woke up with a gasp
when you spoke. *What?* Terrified.
It's okay Daddy. Mom is just talking.
He took it all in at once, my arms around your body
and the room's one dark, that specific speed
at which surprise always falls to the ground.

Gravity's constant. What was the word that woke him?
The only one I think of now is yield.

Little by Little (III)

Little by little the train slows past grass
    the grass

    grows back
(*I am thinking about crickets,* she said,
          grasshoppers . . . all those . . . little things)

Oh, Antigone

        In the field of desire, this tall swath

Little by little through evenings, the red sheets
    like a sultan! says me

and your gold pillow
your eyes, gleaming

      (she's becoming a petal you can look through)
      she's becoming the girl crying

Oh how could I let you—

Hey. Your mother has a question for you.

    The world moving
backward,
the field, swath, low
murmur of tuberose,
shadow on water, a white bridge
       a light
          slows past, by
            little
Are you tired, do you want—
      moving, where
does it hurt, does it feel
      unfamiliar

Here.
Smell this. (the stem
          endless, the bloom
          brown
          with disappearance)

It was the one day
          it was the light, shackling
                           by
little, by
          Drink and be
                   feather-kept
                   petal sheen
                   shaking girl, gone

Mom? Do you have a question for me?

          Drink and be
                   fields, this
                   tall grass, this

Yes.   *My question is*
                   breathing, the white
                        scent-scatter, this
                        endless
                        disappearance
Here.
It was the one bloom,
          it was the bloom cup,
               it was the slim shape
of happiness, *Yes— How*

          and be

Here. Smell this.

Yes.   *My question is*
                         feather-weight, petal
                         shell shape, little
                         bloom last, little
                                        bright
                         and be
                              How
                         and be, anything, *How did*
                         anything
                                        get

                                        so beautiful?

4

The Spring before Spring

Terezin

—a transfer camp in the Czech Republic

We rode the bus out, past fields of sunflowers
that sloped for miles, hill after hill of them blooming.

The bus was filled with old people.
On their laps women held loaves of bread, wrapped in plastic.
Men slept in their seats wearing work clothes.

You stared out the window beside me. Your eyes
were so hard that you might have been watching the glass.

Fields and fields of sunflowers.

Arriving we slowed on the cobblestone walkway.
Graves looked like boxes, or houses from high up.

On a bench teenage lovers slouched in toward each other.
Their backs formed a shape like a seashell.
You didn't want to go inside.

But the rooms sang. Song like breath, blown
through spaces in skin.

The beds were wide boards stacked up high on the walls.
The glass on the door to the toilet was broken.
I imagined nothing.

You wore your black sweater and those dark sunglasses.
You didn't look at me.

The rooms were empty, and the courtyard was empty,
and the sunlight on cobblestone could have been water,
and I think even when we are here we are not here.

The courtyard was flooded with absence.
The tunnel was crowded with light.
Like a throat. Like a—

In a book I read how at its mouth they played music,
some last piece by Wagner or Mozart or Strauss.

I don't know why. I don't know
who walked through the tunnel or who played or what finally
they could have wanted. I don't know where the soul goes.

Your hair looked like wheat. It was gleaming.

Nearby on the hillside a gallows leaned slightly.
What has time asked of it? Nights. Windstorms.

Your hair looked like fire, or honey.
You didn't look at me.

Grass twisted up wild, lit gold all around us.
We could have been lost somewhere, in those funny hills.

And the ride back—I don't remember.
Why was I alone? It was night, then. It was still morning.

But the fields were filled with dead sunflowers.
Blooms darkened to brown, the stalks bowed.
And the tips dried to husks that for miles kept reaching.
Those dreamless sloped fields of traveling husks.

First Love

In this poem there will be no dreaming of spiders.
In this poem there will be no light snow.
It wasn't winter, winter had been cut to shreds
and fed to wolves, they had devoured winter.

There will be no backyards,
nothing will be kept by fence in this poem,
there will be no windows to see the light snow
in the backyard, sudden, without question
although there would never be winter again.
Do you hear me? Never.

In this poem no small hands no cold hands. Don't ask me.
My hands are not cold your hands are not small.
There will be no green cowboy boots in this poem.
You never walked beside me you never smiled no.
There won't be poetry you won't read to me.
There won't be beautiful in this poem.
It was taken on the train with winter. Yes, on the train.
Though there are no trains in this poem and no girls.
No cowboy boots, no rolling windows, the tenements
won't flash blood color through the long afternoons
behind laundry the trees won't shake
the fields will not shine and wait in this poem, no girls.

There will be no letters. The mailbox is being held
without ransom, the white door hangs open all day
on the loose street where winter will never arrive.
Your handwriting will never arrive,
not my name made real by it, no.

There won't be a kiss.
No reeds in the marshland and was it cold, I don't remember.
We won't walk back. There will be no lemon tea, steeped
too long, we pour it down the sink, the cold tea
is dark and strong, my body is being held without ransom.
No not in this poem. There will be no Nina Simone, songs

will not enter songs will not break.
No bedrooms, no postcards on the walls no tulip petals dropping.
There will be no waiting in this poem. There will not be waiting.

Winter is lost forever here, the kidnapped mailbox
long forgotten. The train
is an idea, like the moon. My heart,
searching the street those hours for your tan car,
is a fingernail. Is a hard, shiny, small thing.

Syros, 1989

No woman knows the power she holds at fifteen until it's gone.
Long, loose *S* of the lower back. Inchoate cheekbone,
bracelet of wrist. Soap-soft, uncertain fingertip. Dumb
curve of the bottom lip, stunned to mute by its own prettiness.

I wore a shell-pink dress with a boatneck collar, my long hair
back and up. Limbs dark from days spent propped beside
an ocean blue as eyes of boys we planned to meet.
My best friend Arianne read magazines out loud about

what men want most and whether toothpaste helps bad skin
while we sipped gin and tonics pilfered from the house
her parents kept for weekends out of Athens, though
they never came. We claimed their bougainvillea-splattered deck

with pasta feasts for twenty-five of Arianne's close friends
and left the dishes in what once had been a sink to go out dancing.
Outside the ocean glowed, air dissolved like sugar grains
and even widows sleeping in their black nightgowns dreamed

of the boy with bedspring curls whose first kiss felt like drowning.
That summer everyone was young. In the afternoons I'd wander
down the hill to buy a peach, ro*tha*kino, the word I memorized
to ask for fruit so huge and ripe each peach I've eaten since

has rushed that summer back. The mythically wrinkled man
who sold them in his hut liked to repeat, ro*tha*kino?
to see me blush. Up at the house we halved the pink-gold flesh
and pondered ways to live our lives like movie plots.

Winona Ryder's latest apple-cheeked display of angst
had, in a rage against her mother, drunk too much
and in her mother's makeup teetered up the steeple steps
where yes, the boy with devastating patience was just waiting

to complete her. The church bell, stars, and haloed lantern
he had lit seemed so exactly right that nothing ever need

come after. So when a charmer named Alexandros held out
a lime-tipped gin and tonic at the discotheque and told me

I was beautiful, I smiled mute assent and three nights later
heard myself explain I would go all the way.
No poem could invent the naked woman I watched wade
into the moon-marked water when I made this necessary claim

until I couldn't see her anymore. Even in her bone-white flesh
as firm as bark he'd leaned me up against "to talk" I knew
she wasn't real to anyone but me. And that the pebble-trail
of moonlight she was trying to apprehend would steadily

elude her. It hurt, the way a hip might hit a table in an unlit
room: one quick sharp pain spread slow through the rest of the body.
Then it was over. Mosquito netting swept around the bed,
and just beyond the widened windowsill that sometimes Arianne

camped on, the ocean stayed completely still. (The next night
I would glimpse a hand-sized scorpion on that sill, and watch it
slip into the wall just seconds from her neck's blithe contact
with the sheet.) When Ari's older brothers stumbled in to ask

would I please join them for a drink, Alexandros' mouth above me
yanked into a smile as if connected by a chain to the boys' laughs.
They must have left me there to dress, though all I recollect
is how the tiles shone on every countertop and square of floor

after I cleaned that filthy house for hours. Until the sun came up.
Alexandros returned, to offer dinner and protection rights
he thought he'd earned. The boys and Ari watched while I refused
and heard the offer turn to some excuse about a girl in Athens

he had left behind. I didn't mind. I don't remember what I said
or how I felt beyond relief, or why I made the bet with Arianne
that in our last remaining days of summer break I could seduce
every man named Alexandros on the island. Or what the stakes were.

This is a story about a story. In two weeks I would be sixteen.
This was always a story. I lived each moment of that August
just to tell it, though I never told. The scorpion's quick flight,
the moonlit girl, and how I didn't sleep all night were facts

I stored as IOUs, to be exchanged for Life, that locked-up jewel
much later on. They were my planned escape, before I knew
that time lets fall from trap doors more than anyone would wish.
Or that a story's true as anything. For every fact there is a sly

infinitude of truths, no less for how they contradict. I've left
so many versions out simply to say the word for *peach,*
and that my hair was long. For instance: Alexandros was deaf.
He read my lips, and clipped the edges off the adjectives

he whispered in my ear. Or this: the year that followed Syros
I would sleep with men whose names I didn't know. A story's true
as anything. Fifteen years old. The body still belongs to you.
Not yet a currency with which you pay your way down streets,

and after years will give up like a coat for warmth, or restlessness
or what small muscle love becomes. You want to tell the ones that ask
for more, I'd give that too if it were mine. Maybe it never was.
Maybe I lost only those afternoons of peaches and dry heat

But stories have no stakes, so I don't know. And those slow,
sweet-skinned months when I assumed the moments
I'd accrued would all add up somehow to gloriously cohere,
have disappeared to one dim memory of a room

I never entered. Shadow of a boy's face on the pillow.
Of stone-smooth hips and blindly perfect breasts I watched
with gentle, distant awe, as if my own, and not some
stranger's gaze, were separate from, and longing to come back.

Never

Memory, the crape myrtle's blooming but you won't believe me.
Purr, you don't need it. Year after year, forever.
Tonight on the screen Wendy Darling steps out
on the windowsill, preparing to go. Her toes touch snow.
Never, she says, *is an awfully long time.*

What would you want to believe? We won't go
till we're gone. Never is an awfully long—
kindness of neighbors, of strangers with muffins, I eat each one.
I call the boy I love. Pinching the skin: are you dreaming?
But nobody knows. July is a mess of birthdays: each marked by loss

that's yet to come. *I have a big
question to ask you,* my mother says. *Are my cheeks any smaller?*
I can't seem to remember that the answer doesn't matter.
My lover has a stranger's name. In a month, I tell my mother—
no, in three weeks, you'll be back to your real size.

I wonder as I say it if she'll be alive. If she wonders.
I fit the cap on her jar of cream. White streak under an eye
where it didn't rub in. Hey memory. I told my mom,
I love you, with my head on her chest. *I love you,* she said.
Beside her in the bed my father reading.

He reaches out his hand to fold with hers.
This is a very good hand, my mother says. *I approve of this hand.*
And my father's face like he had made it.
I read poems out loud about God. It's love we won't remember.
I read poems out loud about—cells,

how it's we who make our bodies, not our bodies who make us.
We are bees, the poet says, and the body is a honeycomb.
My mother falls asleep while I am reading, her soft snore.
Mom, are you—? My father nods.
True love, you myth. You ravenous. You won't listen.

On Joy

Last night's rain has filled the fields
with cornflowers, blue-bright as moons
in children's books, all milky light.
They seem, my father says, *the kind of color
that could show up in the night.*

Cornflowers wilt in heat.
By noon the sun will burn the fields
green, as if no bloom had known them.
I picked one to keep, and now
it's the color of paper. My mother's sick.
Today begins her twenty-second day of radiation.
As I write she is strapped to a table
under fourteen floors, face held to a net
of white while instants of light like lead move
through her. I don't know how to say it.

Past these fields are others no one sees,
and past them oak and poplar trees, the evergreen
that slopes up toward a mountain range the same
blue shade and lucid gleam as these quick blooms.
Last night, rain fell in flooded streams.
I tried to wait, but dinner starts at six and by the time
I'd reached the house my dress was slick.
I didn't rush. The drops were warm
and made me laugh, out loud—the laughter's sound
my own, but strange, the way that when
we listen, breath is strange.
As if our loneliness were something I could speak,
when even crickets know we only speak to air.
I want to ask the air, then, how a love
so skilled at longing can become
enough. Why do prayers to no one comfort us?
I want so much. I want a faith I've not
invented, something hard, uncontested as our yard's
wooden table, something that won't ever sound

like my name. Now the afternoon's late.
Light sharpens the skyline like glass in a lens,
making mountains look bluer against where they end.
This light must come from nowhere.

Last night, I walked to dinner on a gravel road
through rain into a joy so unaccountable
and plain, it did not need a witness. But walking back,
the rain had lifted. And in its place, mist drifted low:
a thousand-fingered ghost that seemed to coax
each leaf and blade into a long, inhaled wait,
though what arrival they awaited had already left.
I stopped to watch, but wept.
We've moved for months through hospitals,
learned every name for star-shaped cells
doctors cut from my mother's brain and stained
onto slides before calling us into an office.
Maybe we don't bear the unbearable. Maybe
we die with it. And in our place some larger,
less impatient shape may then be granted space
but I don't want it. I want my mother.

Sometimes beside her in the bed while trying
to tell her I'm okay, I start to weep.
She watches me. Her eyes are distant now,
gone deep inside some gravely gentle place
where, with a stranger's curiosity, she seems to ask
What can I do with your sadness? She has no use for it.
We will lose what we love, and our suffering
is useless, and by dusk all the crickets will thrum
their one absence of warning. That trace of light
against the hills will spread through trees, undo
the ends of evergreen, then fall to fields. It will not hold.
As if it means to urge us, *look*. Love's body must
be manifold. Black cricket shell, new summer air,
late light. The landscape's all ablaze
with gentle strangers. *Look*. We're standing in a field.

Poem to Keep What I Love

> *soon we shall know*
> *if we have learned to accept that the stars*
> *do not go out when we die*
>
> —Abba Kovner

I

Even at dawn while my mother turns
in white quilted sheets for the last peel
of sleep while the dog waits pure of heart
for her door to open, my father
already gone, circling the same blocks
of empty buildings to check wet floors
or new locks, even on Sunday, even
at dawn—the birdsong's all reckless clatter,
stacked against air like metal while cats
hide under ferns and the petal-drunk
cherry trees burn their new beauty to bits.
Spring slides down leaves. Lilacs refuse
every warning. An old man in his good hat
waves without joy and the women follow.
Something falls inside, someone waking,
a new day setting its small systems straight.
Birds insist on themselves. Again *again*
we learn forgetting, practice our goodbyes.

II

In the five minutes between here and there,
Bradford Pears blooming round as balloons
on the clipped blocks of dress shops, framed
chattering white now by trees fat with air.
Poem to keep the Bradford Pears.
Poem to keep sleep, dreams that burrow
under the skin with their knots of questions,
dreams evacuating through the alarm's
blind end. Poem to keep the crowd of light

by the open closet seen only as *light*
upon waking and sourceless. Source
yields ending. Poem to keep five
minutes the sloped fields intact, the cows
unhesitating the blooms fastened to branches
completely. Poem to keep patience
protected. Afloat. Without pull. To keep stars
we can't see from their myth-born explosions
their traveling downward their endless arrival.

III

Against the black spine of fear that travels
through countries, poem, keep what I love.
Against the dreams, which kidnap me.
Against the silk hip of elsewhere, cities of still
swans on black rivers, the lonely nights
mapped neat by the windows of restaurants,
poem, keep what I love. Against days
wound like toys then let loose, painted cars
crashing hard *what I love* though unharmed
into memory. Against freedom's hummed
lilt, tremulous, trapped in the cloaked
sweetness of magnolias at the end of the street,
the front door opening and closing,
its greeting blind *keep* the thumped pulse
of the dog's tail meaning yes, meaning
here and so why won't the green
shutters rack the glass with recognition, why
won't the street turn to water and fall?

IV

After they've left for some other shore where the air
gives off scent like a heat, sweet on the skin and blessed

dumb to the one empty house on its street
in its town where its picture-rich rooms have begun

to collapse. Walls are lungs, losing breath.
Walls are rib cages, necks. Out of duty to grief
the dog's starving to death. And outside—

the world gives itself up like a sham. Departure hangs
loose, quivers bone white in place of the dogwoods.

I am trying to take stock, walk through doorways
before they dissemble. I'm collecting
the colors of windowsills, shutters.

This is the green of new mint. This gold
is the dark gold of nightlights.

Poem bring my love back. Trace the shape
of its absence to being. Polish loss to its starless
immutable sheen. Demand freedom's retreat

from the air inside bones, inside fire, from the air.

V

It isn't unhappiness, this feeling like rain in the bones.

What I love lost to the last farms
at the outer edge of the last towns.
What I love sleeping unawares
while I call to it: fern, jawbone, husk
of the laugh.
Warm fur in the sun, I am calling you.

But what does the dream mean,
the one where everything important is in danger
and my voice gurgles to whispers that no one
but danger can hear—

I want to tell you: this isn't unhappiness.
It's summer.
It's the last good light of the permanent afternoon.
The bay window watching the lake.
It is longing, and longing makes room. And room
makes the breath longer, the love patient and larger.

I want to tell you. Where are you?

VI

When their absence hardens to air.
When their absence is the absence my body leaves.
When I will it gone.

Gone the last day moonlight waiting in milk pods
and gone the ringed oaks dropping dusk onto lawns. Gone
the light piled on doubtful black rooftops, the blithe
blink of lamps spreading outward like palms. And nocturnes,
or opera, blue candle wax sliding, glass table's good-bye dinner
set for the deck. The good-byes caught to collarbones. The last

day lost to sleep. Lost as miracles must be to what we refuse
to remember. Only in grief will love speak through memory:
ribbon-thin language of nomads and thieves. Only in fear will it
shape-shift, trade inherence for accident, the unforeseen.

Come back. We're the birdsong.
Come back. We're the hum of the house at night.
Come back. We're rain, lifting.
Come back. We're the whole of the neighborhood, just loosening.
Just gathering dark.

VII

Surf hum of an air conditioner cools the dark house.
All along the block, honeysuckle drops
scent, and the block takes it. I accept love.

Not its infinity, but its front porch.
All along the block: women at windows
in white nightgowns. Vines climb
a new trellis for air.

The kitchen's dimmed track lights unspool
on the counter, thread magazines loose
till they slip from their stacks.

Water glows from the bottoms of glasses.

And upstairs on a curtain: the yarn hair of lions.
A dragon's green scales are sequins we saved.

Look, it's late.
My mother's still reading on blue
patterned pillows. My father is dreaming of awe.
His head back and mouth tilted upward

and open, as if in his sleep he were trying to catch snow.

VIII

Let me tell you about the honeysuckle
Dense   heavy like water   soon it will be gone

Let me tell you about my mother
Standing in the kitchen

The world dissembles the window slides
Nothing can harm me

Let me tell you about the peonies
White apologies at the edge of yards

Let me tell you how goodbyes arrive
Gray ships on gray water, enormous

Let me tell you about the peonies
How the bloom wants everything

Let me tell you about my mother
Her skin is peonies, honeysuckle, early summer light

one glass of water
one kiss

goodnight

the air collides

IX

yes and the evenings
  my mother says
    the moon!

once it decides
  to get full it gets
    full so quickly

yes love
  keep you yes
    how the sleep

grows sweet
  how the last
    days come

undone without
  regret, this scent
    of honeysuckle

too ripe for regret
  though we dedicate it
    earnestly

The Spring before Spring

I asked my mother, *Will you come sit on my bed?*
This was after I'd walked home in the middle
of streets, afraid of the dark, and after I'd tried
to think of things to tell my grandparents
through a telephone, and they'd tried to think of things
to tell me. My grandmother did not understand
that I was not my mother; her confusion frightened me.
Everyone's suffering comes in moments and then
is forgotten. I gripped my mother's hand.
What is it? she asked. *You don't want to know,* I promised.
I do want to know, she said. *Everyone I love is going to die,*
I told her, and she pulled me into her arms. There, I thought,
it's done. I've given up my secret. She didn't seem to mind.
Love freely, she said, *live in your moment.*
You love me right now. You love me in this moment.
My father walked in wearing his underwear.
Are you modeling, Gabe? my mother asked,
then told him, *We are dealing with death.*
My cheeks were wet. My father kissed me goodnight.
Leaving the room he said, *Remember, we are going to die,*
and we're not going to like it, but it's a good thing,
because then we get to be reborn. We never leave each other.
There's just energy. So when we die we just reconfigure,
we just take different shapes. My mother's mouth dropped.
Om Namah Shivaya, she said. *Umba Gumba Lumba,*
my father answered, and moved his hands around his chest
like a monkey, then told us he loved us and went to bed.
Be grateful for your love, my mother said.
It makes your heart so strong.

Notes

The poem "Letter to Mandelstam" takes its first line from the first line of Mandelstam's poem #354, translated by James Greene. The other two quotations are from "Fourth Prose," an essay written by Mandelstam and translated by Clarence Brown.

The lines my mother reads in "The Winter Before" are from a poem by Hafiz, translated by Daniel Ladinsky.

The title of the third section, "I Have Wished for a Word," was inspired by the poem "After World" by Cecilia Woloch, from her collection of poems entitled *Late*.

The teacher in the poem "To Be, Afraid" is Stanley Plumly, speaking during a seminar on John Keats.

As referenced in "Who Are We That We Come from Somewhere Else:" the fifth circle of Dante's *Inferno* is inhabited by heretics who did not believe in the afterlife. They dwell in tombs of fire, and cannot comprehend the present tense. Whereas in life the future was exactly what they did not know, now in hell they know only the future.

The poem "Little by Little (III)" was partly inspired by Richard Emil Braun's translation of the play *Antigone* by Sophocles, which I use as this collection's epigraph. Used by permission of Oxford University Press, Inc.

The poem also quotes a piece of the last line in Robert Frost's "Directive":

> *Drink and be whole again beyond confusion.*

The epigraph for "Poem to Keep What I Love" is an excerpt from "Detached Verses" from *Sloan-Kettering: Poems* by Abba Kovner, translated by Eddie Levenston, translation copyright © 2002 by the Estate of Abba Kovner Foreword copyright © 2002 by Leon Wieseltier. Used by permission of Schocken Books, a division of Random House, Inc.

In "The Spring before Spring," *Om Namah Shivaya* is a Sanskrit mantra. It can mean: "I honor Shiva, the divine consciousness which is inside of me, and inside of everything."

Acknowledgments

Grateful acknowledgment is made to the editors of the following journals, where poems in this book first appeared:

Antioch Review: "October"; *Crab Orchard Review:* "First Love" and "Mosquito"; *Five Points:* "Letter to Mandelstam"; *Pleiades:* "My Father's Unhappiness" and "In the Afterlife"; *Ploughshares:* "On Joy," "Fugue," "Syros, 1989," and "I Want to Kill the Moths"; *Poetry:* "Poem to Keep What I Love"; *Prairie Schooner:* "To Be, Afraid," "The Last Letter," and "Letter to Have, Letter to Hold"; *Massachusetts Review:* "Letter to Send"

Several people made this book possible. For their mentorship, thank you to Rita Dove, Donald Hall, and Stanley Plumly. For their friendship, thank you to Rita Chin, Jason Koo, Erika Meitner, and Constance Merritt. For love, thank you to my father.

In memory of my mother.

Taije Silverman was raised in Charlottesville, Virginia. Her poetry has been published in journals including *Ploughshares, Poetry,* and *Shenandoah,* and has merited residencies from the MacDowell Colony and the Virginia Center for Creative Arts. Having served as the 2005–2007 Emory University Creative Writing Fellow, Silverman now lives and teaches in Philadelphia.